Our Older
FRIENDS

A Guide for Visitors

Joel T. Keys

FORTRESS PRESS   PHILADELPHIA

Special thanks are in order to M. B. K. for space
and time and encouragement, C. C. for a rich environment, B. H. for some pushes and nudges,
and V. T. for enthusiasm and her delivery service.

Copyright © 1983 by Fortress Press

All rights reserved. No part of this publication may be
reproduced, stored in a retrieval system, or transmitted in any
form or by any means, electronic, mechanical, photocopying,
recording, or otherwise, without the prior permission of the
copyright owner.

———————

Library of Congress Cataloging in Publication Data

Keys, Joel T. (Joel Thompson), 1947–
   Our older friends.

   Bibliography: p.
   1. Aged — Psychology. 2. Visiting the aged.
3. Visiting the sick. 4. Interpersonal relations.
I. Title.
HQ1061.K45   1983   305.2 ′6   83–8865
ISBN 0–8006–1724–X (pbk.)

———————

K363F83   Printed in the United States of America   1–1724

Contents

". . . and some few small aunts, not wanted in the kitchen, nor anywhere else, for that matter, sat on the very edges of their chairs, poised and brittle, afraid to break, like faded tea cups and saucers."

—Dylan Thomas
A Child's Christmas in Wales

Why Share Yourself?

In the midst of the unfamiliar it is easy to lose our bearings and not live to our potential.

Imagine a family from colonial times transported to the twentieth century and given a nice suburban home in which to live. How quickly would they learn about and adapt to that environment? How soon would they start cooking on the stove in the kitchen instead of in the fireplace in the den? How quickly would they give up using the ornamental candles in the dining room and begin using the electric lights? When would they plug the vacuum cleaner cord into a socket instead of using it to tether a dog or a calf? Certainly the process of adaptation would be a frustrating experience for our friends, an experience in which they would realize their potential for living very slowly. Undoubtedly the adjustment time would be shortened greatly if they had a guide along who could point out the modern conveniences and tell how they operate. Even an instruction manual or a guidebook to the house would help.

In our experiences with the elderly too often we find ourselves in situations where, with all good intentions and intelligence, we are in a new and unfamiliar world. Only very slowly do we find our way; only very slowly are we able to care in the ways we really need to care. Even though we are surrounded by resources, we may never see or use them. The result is a bad or lukewarm

experience, one that never reaches its potential in terms
of human growth, wholeness, and dignity.

The purpose of this book is to provide a guide for you
as you experience and spend time with older, often invalid persons. It will help you know what to expect of
the environment in which you find a particular older
friend as well as give you some ideas as to how that environment affects that person. This book will also help
you know what to expect from yourself. It will help you
provide a better experience for that elderly person with
whom you will share some very special time. Hopefully,
what you read will also help your relationship become
more satisfying to you.

Perhaps you are concerned about an older family
member, neighbor, or friend. Or perhaps you are part
of a program that seeks to offer special attention and
care to elderly, invalid persons. Regardless of the circumstances that have brought about your concern, keep
in mind that when you build a relationship with an
older person, especially one whose mobility is in one
way or another restricted, you are becoming involved
with a person who is living in a crisis situation.

In the biblical sense a crisis occurs any time a major
decision, judgment, or event takes place in a person's
life. A crisis can result in growth and progress to
wholeness, or it can bring about pain, fragmentation,
and alienation. The particular crises of older persons are
as different as the people themselves. They can be
brought about by a single factor or by a combination of
physical, emotional, financial, spiritual, or relationship
factors. Yet whatever the crisis situation, the elderly
often desperately need to talk with someone who is sen-

sitive, concerned, and skilled in relating to their problems.

This book cannot replace your own experiences, your own sensitivity and awareness, your efforts at continuing to learn and grow. However, it can be used to enhance your relationships with older persons. You may use this book as you wish. Some of the material contained herein will make sense immediately. Other parts will have validity only after more experience in the relationship, so you might wish to thumb through this book periodically as the relationship continues.

Why share your time and yourself with the elderly? The wholeness and dignity of another human being can be positively affected by your presence and person. You can be a source of strength to another! For it is in the meeting of souls that loneliness is banished, in the sharing of pain, whether physical or emotional, that pain becomes bearable. Fear that is expressed tends to dissipate. When the warmth of a hand is felt, the warmth of a heart grows. You have gifts to give, or better you have gifts to *be* for someone else.

Qualities of a Good Visitor

ONE EVENING a physician friend of mine reflected on the first ten years of his medical practice. He said that he had felt frustration in his vocation until he began to get involved with his patients. "At first I was a technician. 'For pneumonia do this; for gall bladder trouble do that.' Then I found I had more to give than medication. I could give myself. When you get right down to it, that's all any of us have to give — ourselves."

In a relationship all you need to give is yourself. In truth, all you *can* give is yourself. Yet giving ourselves away is not an easy task. This is true in any relationship, but in our relationships with invalid and older persons there are some particular dynamics at work that make sharing ourselves harder. We bring into these relationships our fears about our own aging and our own infirmities, present or yet to come. A friend once refused to visit in a nursing home, telling me, "I can't go into those places. I'm too afraid of ending up in one myself." Our body, our pains, our death can be called to consciousness when we are faced with persons whose frailty and mortality seem to be the primary marks of their existence.

We could block out all these thoughts and feelings. We could try to suppress them. Those are very natural reactions. But in hiding from our fears we prevent growth in facing our finitude, and we are paralyzed when we must respond to others for whom the issues of aging, frailty, and death are even more pressing.

Whether we are conscious of it or not, each time we encounter older people we carry with us feelings and experiences from prior relationships with grandparents, parents, or parent figures we have known. Failure to acknowledge this dynamic causes us to relate to our present elderly friends in many of the same patterns and ways we related to the persons in our past. Thus, the people we share our time with today are not allowed to truly be themselves.

Listening to ourselves, to what our hearts and minds are saying, is an essential ingredient in becoming people who can give of themselves to the elderly. Listening to what is happening within us and being able to tag those thoughts and feelings can free us from bondage to them. For example, you may have heard someone say "I was more scared when I didn't know what disease I had. Now that I know what it is, I know I have a rough road ahead, but at least I *know*." For that person, naming the ailment has taken away some of its power. If you and I can name those fears, those unresolved aspects of who we are, then they lose much of their power over us.

Knowing what our hang-ups are frees us to use them as bridges to sharing in someone else's plight. For us to say "I'm scared of dying, too" in response to a fear expressed by a friend may do more for the bonds of the relationship than any sugarcoated "there-there" could ever hope to produce.

We bring to our relationships with invalid and elderly persons years of hopes and fears, triumphs and failures, joys and sorrows. The key is to let all these things work for, not against, us in relationships. If we deny them they will have power over us, and they will prevent us from truly being ourselves. But if we use our experiences as tools in building relationships, we lay claim to a gift. We transform pain into new life.

Be aware of your motivation in caring for an invalid and elderly person. If that person is a relative, understand how guilt may or may not be at work. If that person is a neighbor, acquaintance, or someone you have met through a church or community visitation program, be certain of why you have become involved. Is it because you just want to do something nice for someone less fortunate than yourself? Perhaps it is a way of facing and dealing with your own fears about aging and death. Or maybe you are concerned because you have parents who are miles away, for whom you can do little on a daily or weekly or monthly basis, and you want to do something for an older person geographically closer to you.

To know your own motivation in caring for an older person enables you to become aware of what it is you hope to gain from the relationship. After all, there is nothing wrong with having your own needs met through visiting with and caring for an elderly person, just as long as it does not get in the way of meeting that person's needs.

Knowing precisely and specifically what your motivations are will lead to knowing what you can reasonably expect from yourself. In examining those expectations you can become much more realistic, thereby avoiding much frustration. I believe that all of human life involves learning what is within our abilities and control and what lies beyond our abilities and control. A relationship with an invalid and older person is in a sense a microcosm of that learning which takes place throughout our pilgrimage.

For example, to expect that you will be able to help a person cope emotionally with encroaching blindness is an unreal expectation. But to expect that you will try to be an open person who will listen to concerns about loss of sight, who will openly share feelings about such loss, and who will be present with and for the older person during this experience is much more realistic. (And bound to be much less frustrating as well!)

Knowing those limits is of primary importance in caring for yourself. You cannot banish aging's results. You cannot take away physical infirmity. You cannot by yourself change the sociological or institutional problems that involve aging in this century and in this society. To fail to know one's limits can make the relationship a difficult experience.

If in caring for an older person you find yourself feeling that you are not getting anywhere or that the relationship seems to be something less than fulfilling, ask yourself: "Just what do I expect? What do I expect of myself? What do I expect of this other person?" Granted, our reach should always exceed our grasp, but we must be careful that the expectation of our grasp not exceed the potential. Success, greatness, and rewards are found by working for realizable dreams, not for castles in the clouds.

The specific living out of reaching *to* but not *beyond* our abilities must involve setting some very precise limits on how you will and will not function with your elderly friend. You may wish to try and set some limits today. You can always adjust and alter them later. For example, you may decide that you can spend only one hour (or even less) each time you encounter this person. You may decide that you will not (or will) run errands. Then you must stick to the discipline you have set. It may sound heartless and coldblooded, but in the long run it will add to the quality of your experience.

Some older persons will cling to you, having very unrealistic expectations of your relationship. You cannot spend twenty-four hours of every day with your elderly friend. You cannot meet that person's every desire and need. But you can offer to share yourself, and you will do that better if you have set some limits to the nuts-and-bolts, day-to-day structure of the relationship.

Unconsciously we provide structure for all our relationships. We all create limits in our dealings with others, but those limits are often unspoken and thus often overlooked. For a variety of reasons relationships with our older friends are a bit more complicated and difficult and so require a bit more definition and clarity of structure.

You have within yourself some qualities, either developed or potential, that need to be exercised if the relationship you have with an elderly person is to grow and progress and yield the fruits that can be brought forth by two human beings spending time together.

THE ABILITY TO LISTEN

In order to be helpful to other people we must be able to create space for them. We must be open to who they are and to what they think and feel. We must be able to meet them where they are as opposed to where we think they ought to be. Within ourselves we need to develop a spirit of nonjudgmental presence. This gives other people the right to think and feel and be what they want to be.

We live in a society of "fixers" and problem solvers. When a child has a skinned knee we try and make it better. And if we cannot make it better, then we try to deny there is a problem by telling the child that it doesn't really hurt. Likewise, when one of our older friends offers a complaint, it is our tendency to either fix the problem, no matter how impossible that might be, or to avoid and deny the problem. Furthermore, we try to be practical people who deal with facts and with what we perceive as the truth. Thus, when an older friend offers an opinion based on a perception of the world that does not fit our perception of the world, there is a tendency to try and correct that bit of "misinformation," even when it is very subjective. "The food in this place is bad," she says, and we respond, "Oh, it's not that bad. It looks pretty good."

Good listening means creating space for that other person. One must try to avoid evaluating and correcting and instead accept what that other person says as a valid expression of thoughts and feelings and personhood. We may try to deny guilt, helplessness, or anger and sugarcoat things, but that does little to create that all-important space for that all-important other person.

Being a good listener does not exclude being a talker. But it does mean that when we talk we respond to what we have heard from the other person, verbally as well as nonverbally. Thus, we have to "listen" with our eyes as well as with our ears, always trying to understand our tendency to filter and distort what we hear and see.

BEING OPEN TO OURSELVES

The ability to listen to oneself and to learn new and wonderful things is a beautiful gift. From the cradle to the grave life involves a long search for identity. As we progress in time and experience new layers are peeled back, new aspects shine forth, new revelations appear. All of these dynamics continue to our death.

Reaching a certain age hands out no automatic merit badge for growth or self-knowledge. Nor does attaining a particular time or station in life give anyone a certain fixed point from which the rest of life can be lived without fear or risk or questioning. Once I asked some teenagers to draw symbols of the most significant times in a person's life. The results of this exercise showed a perception that from birth to age twenty-five a person encounters much growth and change and struggle; after age twenty-five there may be one or two significant events, but nothing that amounts to much! The truth is that we are constantly growing and changing, facing new challenges and learning new things about our constantly new selves.

We are deep and complicated creatures. There is much substance to us. Sometimes we may like what we see; other times we may deny or try to run from what we find within ourselves. But at all times it is important to be open to listening to what we are thinking and feeling and saying in our relationships with elderly friends.

THE WILLINGNESS TO LEARN

You must be committed to learning when in a relationship with an elderly person. Basically, you have access to two kinds of resources that can aid learning.

Information. Books, television, magazines, and people can supply you with information about the variety of aspects of aging and invalidism that presents itself to you. By keeping in touch with current thinking and methodology among professionals who work with the aging, by keeping abreast of sociological trends, and by keeping before you the issues that are raised by the phenomenon of aging, you will find yourself more sensitive to that older person. Disparate pieces of the puzzle of your relationship will suddenly fit together. Information gathering will also help you realize that you are not the only person in the world faced with the particular joys and frustrations of sharing life with a person in the crisis of aging.

Experience. Reflection upon your own experience with your elderly friend brings a more personal kind of learning. You, a unique person, are spending time with another unique person at a particular point in time in a particular setting. It is hard to generalize about that! Thus, thinking back over your visiting experience brings learning which is more applicable to the parties involved. Asking what did he or she say, verbally and nonverbally, and how did I respond to that? brings an understanding that gets at the very heart of whether or not you are truly creating space for the other person, whether or not you are doing what you set out to do.

When should reflection occur? Whenever it's best for you. For example, I have several intersections at which I have long waits for the signal to turn green. It is at these places that I have found I do my best reflection after visiting in the hospital. Whatever the case, it is important to learn from your visiting experience.

DEPENDABILITY

Your commitment to that other person requires that you be dependable. All of us at one time or another have been stood up for appointments. When we finally decided that the other person was not going to arrive, we may have muttered a few mild oaths under our breath then found something else to do. Your friend is likely to be planning for your visit, waiting for your promised phone call or card. If you fail to follow through, that person has little else to do. Living up to promises and schedules is important. No more need be said about that.

You are a unique person with a multiplicity of gifts, known and yet to be revealed. You have the potential to be a very important person in the life of someone else. In the realization of that potential you, too, can grow and learn.

You will find that the most difficult task we face in all relationships is how to be ourselves and how to let other people be themselves. You will also find that we can never perfect that. At least not in this life. But we can share in the pilgrimage of discovery and of intimacy by caring both for ourselves and for our older friends.

The Elderly's Environment

YOUR RELATIONSHIP with an older person unfolds, like all relationships, in a particular environment. The skilled or intermediate-care nursing home, the retirement home, and the private residence each has its particular characteristics. Likewise, there are some similarities. The quirks and foibles of each are discussed below. This information will help prepare you for your visits and will give you some insight into your older friend's living environment. Though your central concern might be someone who lives at home, there may be some helpful information in the other sections, so skipping over seemingly irrelevant material is against the rules!

NURSING HOMES

The nursing home as a widely used and accepted institution is a relatively recent addition to the American cultural scene. The elderly poor were cared for in Europe by means of almshouses created by the church during the Middle Ages. In more recent history the almshouses were taken over by communities. However, these institutions were for the poor; families provided most care for the aged.[1]

By the 1920s nursing and retirement facilities existed for persons of particular professions. The Royal Chelsea Hospital, still operating in London, was created for British military men. Nursing homes and retirement facilities for sailors and members of fraternal orders and even places such as the actors' home portrayed in Neil Simon's *The Sunshine Boys* were typical of that period. But the nursing home was not the widely experienced institution that it is today.

A change in the American cultural and economic scenes has produced several phenomena which have increased the need for nursing homes. First, we have changed from a culture and economy that was agrarian, rural, and small family to one that is industrial, technological, and urban and suburban. This has effected a change in the character of the family unit. Because our economy demands mobility and because housing patterns have changed, no longer are aunts, uncles, grandmothers, grandfathers, and other family members necessarily lifelong residents on the family property. In the past the family was an extended unit which included a number of generations. Now the two-generation nuclear family is the norm, thus changing housing patterns and needs. Smaller homes and more frequent moves have modified relationships with older family members. Highly mobile children leave the older generation, who often desire to remain in familiar communities near old friends, in touch with their church, clubs, and sense of home.

The second ingredient in the increase of nursing homes involves recent advances in medical technology which have caused more people to live longer. Treatment of invalid and elderly persons often requires skills possessed by trained personnel only. Finding skilled persons to provide home care is practically impossible. Or, if such personnel is found, the cost is prohibitive. The reasonable and economical answer to providing this new medical care is the nursing home, where staff and services are assembled at one site and used by a number of different persons.

Advances in medical technology have their negative side. We become concerned with maintaining life without considering the quality of that life. Some nursing homes and their staffs and attending physicians are able to understand and face this issue, others are not. Too often death, even in the elderly, is seen as a failure to persons whose training has taught them that their sole purpose is to cure. Disease is reversible in many cases, aging is not.[2]

It was during the Depression that our society as a whole began to look after the care of the invalid and elderly person. The rise of the social security system in this era is one indication of this.[3] Furthermore, in the decades following the Depression, rapid growth in the use and number of nursing homes occurred. In 1939 there were twelve hundred nursing homes operating in the United States;[4] in 1977 there were nearly twenty-five thousand,[5] an increase of about two thousand percent in less than forty years. At present approximately four to five percent of persons over age sixty-five are in institutions, though this figure, which equals almost one million people, is misleading since it represents only those in nursing homes at a specific time and does not account for those who are in and out at different intervals.[6] It is difficult to generalize about nursing homes because their sponsorship and management vary greatly. Eighty percent are commercial,[7] which means that the nursing-home business is big business. Churches, governments, and other organizations sponsor the remainder.

Your impressions of different nursing homes will run

the spectrum of seeing the home as a hospital, a nice
hotel, a college dormitory, or simply as a warehouse for
storing the infirm. Persons unfamiliar with the nursing-
home environment will be affected by their first visit.
Below are listed several situations you might encounter
upon visiting a nursing home. Do not be unduly surprised; they are normal situations, and you are normal
if they catch your attention during your visit!

The Residents. Upon entering you may see a number
of residents sitting around, doing nothing, going
nowhere. These persons are at a variety of consciousness levels and in a variety of physical states.
Some may be bright and communicative, others dour
and silent. Still others may moan, mutter, or talk to
themselves. Some may be asleep. Clothing and posture
may vary, with both hospital gowns and street clothes
evident. Heads may be slumped or tilted. Some of the
residents may be strapped into chairs or wheelchairs by
means of harnesses or towels. Despite the visual picture
you encounter, it is important to remember that these
people vary from your humanity in form only and not
in essence.

Medical Environment. The nursing home has a strong
medical atmosphere, which to most of us is mysterious
and alien. However, there appears to be less treatment
and activity here than in a hospital. Uniformed nurses
and aides may be present, medical terminology may be
used on door signs or at ward desks, and medical equipment — wheelchairs, respirators, hospital beds, and bed-
pans — may be within view, but not many "cures" are
being effected.

Smells. We forget our olfactory sense — until it encounters something new or unpleasant. The nursing

home will have an odor to it, be that odor the aroma of medicine, urine, institutional food, or carpet shampoo.

The Staff. The staffs of nursing homes vary in intelligence, diligence, attitude, and energy, just like the staffs of any business or institution. Of course a well-managed nursing home attracts employees of better skill and dedication, but there are bound to be personnel problems in every institution. The work can be depressing, the pay is often low, and the demands made by those residents who seek individualized attention make for a difficult work situation. It is no wonder that the turnover on nursing-home staffs is extremely high. This turnover means that there are fewer old hands around who have a feeling of pride or of investment in the institution. Also, the turnover means that the residents have fewer long-term relationships with staff members. The staff, then, has the tendency to be employees instead of friends.

Among the staff there are the good eggs and the bad eggs. There are people who truly care about the patients, and there are those who are merely putting in time to draw a paycheck. Staff strength or weakness can be difficult to discern. Residents may complain of theft of personal items, but quite often the missing object has been mislaid or was never brought to the nursing home in the first place. The resident may complain about the staff never answering the buzzer that is supposed to summon a nurse or aide, but one must remember that the slowness of response seems longer when one's days are relatively unoccupied or when a proud adult needs assistance in answering "the call of nature."

After awhile a visitor can begin to distinguish the strengths and weaknesses of a particular nursing home's staff. A visitor will discover some problems are related to the quality of the staff, while others are related to the staff's limited size. One can empathize with a nursing home trying to beat inflation and ever-increasing medical costs. After all, the person paying the bills is the beneficiary. However, it is difficult to empathize with lack of concern or incompetence.

Good lines of communication between you and the staff of a nursing home can be an important ingredient in making your involvement happier and more effective. You may be quite surprised by the knowledge and concern that staff members exhibit when they notice your own knowledge and concern about a particular resident. Also, there might be good reason why a particular resident gets a certain kind of treatment. For example, I had a friend who complained of the nurses' failure to dress her each morning. The social worker in that nursing home explained that ignoring my friend's requests to be dressed was part of an intentional program to make her become more self-sufficient. The program seemed to work for each day my friend would end up dressing herself!

It is good to know the personnel entrusted with the care of the person you visit!

RETIREMENT HOMES AND COMPLEXES

Many of the changes in cultural patterns that precipitated the increase of nursing homes have also influenced the growth of institutional retirement residences. In addition, the work and expense involved in maintaining a private residence has had an effect on housing patterns of the elderly.

Retirement homes or complexes may be high-rise

buildings, cottages, duplexes, hotel-type accommodations, or a combination of any of these. Like nursing homes, retirement facilities cover a wide spectrum in terms of beauty and repair. Some are unusually plush and are inhabited by persons of above-average financial means. This state of comfort is not universal, of course, and other, less luxurious, complexes tend to be more depressing to both the visitor and the resident. As a result, in a retirement facility you might encounter spacious, carpeted lobbies and lovely antiques and chandeliers or dark halls, peeling paint, and dusty floors.

Regardless of the luxury or lack thereof found within, retirement complexes generally provide their residents with a variety of activities and opportunities for social interaction. Bingo, cards, worship, field trips, and cocktail parties bring the residents together. The problems of cooking for one are solved by common dining facilities, thus providing another common meeting ground. Transportation for shopping trips, doctors' appointments, and community cultural events usually is available through the institution.

Sponsorship of retirement facilities may rest with a commercial enterprise, a religious body, or a community. Those sponsored by religious bodies may or may not restrict residency to those of the same faith. Frequently tied to sponsorship is the availability of volunteers, who often enhance the residents' quality of life.

In general, retirement complexes offer a homier atmosphere than do nursing homes. Residents are allowed to furnish their rooms or apartments with their own belongings. There are often options in decoration, room arrangement, and appliances. One friend in her eighties explained with great glee how she had been forced to rearrange her whole kitchen area in order to accommodate her wet bar! In some retirement complexes individual kitchens provide the option of cooking for oneself, thereby enabling the residents to take periodic breaks from the routine of the dining room. In other retirement homes kitchen facilities may be an area set aside on each hall and shared by a number of residents.

Retirement complexes require a greater degree of self-sufficiency on the part of their residents than do nursing homes. Nursing care may be available through an infirmary or through a cooperative plan with another local institution, but generally good health and mobility is a requirement for entry into a retirement home.

Two sociological subtleties exist in most retirement complexes. The first of these has to do with the fact that many residents have few, if any, cross-generational experiences. Card games, shopping trips, and meals are shared with persons of the same age group. Therefore, when children visit a retirement facility they may be either ignored or "attacked"! I remember a parallel situation from college. For six days a week I was cloistered with young adults, but on Sundays I encountered numbers of smaller creatures who both delighted me and put utter terror into my heart. The same sort of distortion of normal life exists in the retirement complex.

The second of the subtleties has to do with who goes to which retirement facility. Usually there is a great deal of choice involved, whereas nursing-home choice is limited by the availability of beds and the urgency of the crisis that created the need for nursing care. The choice of a particular retirement facility is often based upon who already lives there. Friends and family tend to congregate at one institution. As people begin to think of themselves moving to a retirement facility, they frequently envision themselves in a setting where their acquaintances have moved. This dynamic means that when some retirement facilities first open their doors, they are involved in a desperate financial struggle for a year or two, until a few key people choose to move in. After that the residence fills rapidly and soon boasts a waiting list. While the social aspect is positive in that it creates an opportunity for continuing long-term relationships, it also creates the possibility of cliques and hurt feelings. Rejections that you and I would call minor tend to balloon and become exaggerated in the institutional setting where people are together meal after meal, bridge game after bridge game, church service after church service.

PRIVATE RESIDENCES

Invalid and elderly persons may live in a house or an apartment in any kind of neighborhood. This residence may be the person's own home, or it may be the home of a family member or friend. Contact with neighbors cannot be assumed, but frequently, especially in close-knit neighborhoods where the people have a common history, the neighbors provide some care and emotional support for invalid and elderly persons and cross-generational relationships are able to develop.[8] Also, visiting nurses, housekeepers, or other persons often provide frequent social experiences for the private resident.

However, an elderly person in a private home can have a hermitlike existence. The resident can withdraw from any contact with the outside world, making those who wish to visit feel reticent since the private home is very clearly someone else's turf.

Most private homes are not equipped for invalids. Stairs present problems. Special equipment may be necessary for bathing. Physical and psychological changes associated with aging increase the likelihood of accidents in the home. Poor eyesight and weak muscles can contribute to accidents in the bathroom, around steps, and in the kitchen.

The homebound are more susceptible to assault, robbery, and con artists. Almost every Christmas the newspapers carry stories about an older person living on a limited income getting flimflammed. Regardless of the neighborhood, the elderly person living alone too often falls prey to criminals.

Rocky relationships can result when family or friends begin to feel trapped in caring for the homebound. Quite often these care givers catch the brunt of the resident's anger at becoming dependent and immobile.

Yet the familiar surroundings of a private home, the sense of pride and self-sufficiency gained by maintaining one's own residence, and the opportunity for continued contact with a variety of people on a day-to-day basis make the private residence very attractive to the person who is physically, psychologically, and financially able to remain there.

Our Older Friends

IT IS IMPORTANT to avoid stereotypes when dealing with people. Invalid and older persons, whether living at home or in institutions, are no exceptions. Each person has a unique makeup of genes, life experience, physiology, outlook, strength, and frailty.

What follows is a discussion of general patterns and tendencies of elderly people. It is not to be taken as a description of any one person or as the answer to questions you have about your elderly friend. The information is provided instead as a reference so that you might understand the complexity of the person you visit and some of the dynamics of aging in general. Hopefully, it will heighten your sensitivity to multiple facets of the aging experience affecting your friend. Use the information to keep your eyes, ears, and heart open to the variety of factors that contribute to your friend's life situation. Do not let data, facts, and statistics presented here or anywhere else get in the way of clearly seeing your older friend. You need to be counted as someone special and unique; so does your friend.

At a seminar on aging I was asked by a college student: "What are the needs of the invalid and elderly?" The answer came in a question posed to him: "What are *your* needs?" People are people, and our primary needs remain the same. We have basic physiological needs. We have a need for identity, for value and dignity.

Finally, we all share the needs to love and be loved and
to find community and purpose for our lives.

But invalid and elderly people are different from most
of us in that their needs are less likely to be met.
Physiological needs change with aging; increased
medical care must be paid for from a decreased income,
which can cause great concern. It is hard to fill the need
for identity in institutions that take away one's choice of
food, decor, clothing, and activities. The need for a
sense of value and dignity can go unmet when a person
is treated as an object of technology rather than as a
human being. The needs to love and be loved and to
find community and purpose remain unfulfilled when
isolation, the loss of friends and abilities, and depression invade a formerly active, vibrant human being.

None of the factors that comprise the experience of
human life can be removed from their context;
physiology, rationality, our emotional being, our relationships, our spirituality are all intertwined. When one
aspect of our being is adversely affected, there is bound
to be an effect on the other aspects. Sometimes an
assault on one part means that another part will compensate and come to the rescue, as in the case of coping
with a physical illness by relying on spiritual strength.
Or, on the other hand, when one aspect of a person is
adversely affected, the other aspects may be injured as
well. Immediately after an emotional shock we tend not
to be very rational nor do we digest our food well.

Despite the fact that the following information is
divided into separate classifications, please remember
that all facets are inextricably woven together. The divi-
sion below is purely for clarity. It is provided to help
you think about the possible crises of your older friend

in some orderly fashion. Also remember that you are dealing with a unique person who is complex and more than the sum of his or her parts.

PHYSIOLOGY OF THE ELDERLY

While there are some general physiological character-istics of aging, it is important to be aware that each per-son has a unique history of diseases and accidents. Recognizing this helps us view an invalid, older person as an individual rather than as a geriatric case.

Neurological Changes. Aging brings about neuro-logical changes in us. The brain weight of a person at age seventy-five is about fifty-six percent of the normal adult weight.[1] However, with the decrease in weight comes a compensation which provides for the brain's continuation of active functioning. Also, we normally only use a small percentage of our brains, so the change is not as drastic as it sounds. Certainly changes in the brain take their toll on sensory, motor, and rational abilities. Testing has shown that responses to stimuli may be slowed with aging but that accuracy of responses does not deteriorate.[2]

Body Chemistry. Aging can bring on rapid changes in body chemistry. As in adolescence and menopause, the advanced stages of aging can produce imbalances that cause more than physiological effects. If body chemistry is in constant flux, medication is more difficult to prescribe and manage. For example, some medications require time to build up in the body's system, so physi-cians may be required to spend weeks trying to find the drug with the least number of side effects for a par-ticular person. Relief from pain or other physical ail-ments is thus delayed.

The Senses. The senses tend to become impaired and less efficient during the normal progress of aging. Since the senses are our contact with the outside world, the effects are more than physiological.

Hearing is the sense affected most by the processes of aging. Fifty percent of the males and thirty percent of the females over age sixty-five experience a hearing loss that impairs social interaction.[3] Note the following, supposedly true, anecdote:

> Living in a church-sponsored retirement home in a large southern city are two genteel ladies who have been lifelong friends. They were born and raised in the same neighborhood, went through elementary and boarding school together, and were suite mates in college. After both had married, they moved into the same neighborhood and raised their families down the street from each other. Their husbands died within months of each other, and so these ladies decided to move into the same retirement home. In short, their history together was long, and the bonds between the two were deep.
>
> One day, after a long and exhausting shopping trip into the downtown area, the two lifelong friends stood waiting for the elevator to take them to their respective floors. One turned to the other and said, "I'm tired. Aren't you?" Her friend turned to her and said, "I'm tired of you, too!" And the two have not spoken since.

Often older persons are accused of selective hearing, hearing only what they want to hear, when in fact they may have problems with certain sound frequencies. In large crowds where there is a dull roar providing a background noise, "masking," or confusion of articulation and discrimination of sound, may occur.[4] The decibels may be adequate, but the listener hears only garbled sounds that do not distinguish themselves as syllables, vowels, or consonants. Thus, deafness is not necessarily total. It can come and go with the particular setting and sound.

We take for granted our senses of smell and taste. They are perfect examples of "not missing our water until the well has run dry." The impairment or deterioration of these two interrelated senses may be the source of complaints about food,[5] resulting in loss of appetite and displeasure in eating. Or the person who has experienced loss of taste and smell may engage in massive eating, trying to find some semblance of taste.[6]

The sense of sight can also be adversely affected by the aging process. By far the most common visual impairment associated with aging is farsightedness. One friend claimed that there was "nothing wrong with my eyes that lengthening my arms wouldn't cure." As aging advances pupils begin to react slower in their adjustment to light and dark, causing night blindness to occur. Cataracts and glaucoma are more common in older persons than in the general population. Medical advances in treating these conditions are being made, but treatment is not readily available everywhere. Sometimes the nature of the particular impairment may not be treatable, or the person's general health may preclude treatment. The result, then, is that one older person may have a very real hope for improvement in eyesight while another faces only further deterioration.

Impaired vision detracts from a person's ability to function. The possibility for accidents from falls exists as does the possibility of misreading labels on medicine bottles, resulting in either the wrong dosage or the wrong medicine. Also, some older persons experience

disorientation and confusion after dark. This phenomenon, called "sundowning," may be the result of changes
in the amount of light stimulus, which would go un-
noticed by persons in normal circumstances.

Finally, the elderly's sense of touch or feeling may be
impaired. This can have two different manifestations.
The first involves the inability to discriminate between
hot and cold or sharpness and bluntness. The second involves a loss in the ability to sense body position. A person sitting in a chair may be less aware of the exact position of legs and feet, and so, when attempting to stand,
stumbles and falls. The deterioration of the sense of
touch increases the likelihood of broken bones, bumps
on the head, and other accidents. The elderly's weak
muscles and brittle bones respond more slowly to prevent an accident and also recover more slowly after an
accident has occurred.

EMOTIONAL ASPECTS OF AGING

The experience of being invalid and elderly can bring
emotional pain. The limitations with which the individual lives make it difficult to cope with much that
goes on.

Change. Change in our culture is fast and pervasive.
It takes much emotional energy in order to cope with
change. Moving, a new job, a death in the family, the
addition of a new child — all of these things, whether
good or bad, affect us emotionally and require the exer-
cising of emotional "muscles" in order to adjust. Older
persons experience changes which are greater in number
and more devastating in effect than those experienced
by any other age group. The turmoil of adolescence
seems almost trivial compared to the changes experienced daily by our older friends.

A great deal of emotional energy is required to deal with changes in one's body. Disease and deterioration, whether sudden or gradual, can bring about a "what's-the-use" attitude in the elderly or a loss of a sense of self. In a culture which is amazed when a thirty-three-year-old woman can be a successful model, it is difficult to see lines, wrinkles, and cracks appear; it is difficult to have one's body take such radical turns in the way it functions. Physical change makes us feel out of control, less of a person.

Our older friends may seem at times like hypochondriacs. They may seem totally preoccupied with the functioning of their bodies and with what we consider to be normal aches and pains.[7] But it is normal that what was once a source of relative certainty but now is a source of change should become an obsession. Especially when each change or ache is symbolic of mortality and finitude.

There is much change outside the invalid and older person. Besides the changes that all of society faces, older people who live with their children must face and adjust to changes in the life of their "caretakers." Those changes might be as big as a move to another city or as tiny as the addition of a new puppy to the family unit.

A move to a retirement home or a nursing home requires great adjustment. It is more than a relocation of one's home, as the following example illustrates.

When I first saw the lady she was lying in her bed in the hospital. She was jaundiced. Her face was drawn in an expression of utter terror, her eyes wide open with fear. "What's wrong?" I asked. "They're going to move me to D Building," she said. I looked puzzled. "You don't know what D Building is?" she asked, indicating that I must be some kind of fool not to know what D Building was.

I knew that D Building was the chronic care part of the medical complex, but it was obvious that it must be something more than that. "No, I don't know what D Building is. Tell me."

She raised up slightly in the bed, drew her index finger symbolically across her throat in jugular-slitting fashion, and said very, very conclusively, "D Building. That means *curtains.*"

The highest mortality rate in nursing homes occurs during the first year of residence.[8] While that is due in part to a high rate of acute physical illness, the trauma brought on by the move to a nursing home contributes as well. Those residents who best cope with the change are often the active, aggressive type,[9] those who are able to martial their emotional and spiritual resources and face the big change in life style.

Sometimes a period occurs during which people decide whether or not to make the adjustment. If they decide not to completely accept the new setting, they may go through a variety of internal changes. They may become angry and hostile toward staff and visitors. They may find another, happier, "reality." Or they may decide to give up and die.

August. Mrs. E was ninety-five and had just come to the nursing home after suffering several strokes. As I talked with the social worker at the nursing home I was impressed by her realistic approach. "This is not Mrs. E's apartment, and she will not live like she did in her apartment. This place is not the most wonderful place in the world. The question for Mrs. E is: 'What will she do with her time here?' She may cope somehow or another, or she may decide to die."

December. Mrs. E, a well-educated, well-traveled, reserved lady, made friends with a gentleman of the same

background. "He's awfully young, but is a wonderful con-
versationalist," she said. The septuagenarian would push
her wheelchair for her; she was the first person with
whom he had been able to converse daily since he had
entered the nursing home six months before. Mrs. E was
trying to find something worth living for.

February. Mrs. E had withdrawn. She rarely came out of
her room. The social worker said, "I think she's decided to
die. But at least she tried." I nodded in agreement.

August. Mrs. E died. "At ninety-six years old her body
was still in such good shape that it took her from February
until now to die," the social worker said.

Change is difficult because it means loss: loss of
physical attributes, loss of the ability to perform routine
as well as more challenging activities, loss of a familiar
environment, loss of dignity, loss of a sense of self. On
top of these changes come the grievous deaths of friends
and family, a constant reminder to the elderly that one
day they, too, will die.

Elderly people see themselves in an unfamiliar world.
They see wars brought into the living room via the
television. They see changes in morality, social struc-
tures, and religion. Our nation's elderly come from a
generation that stressed reserve and dignity.[10] They
have a need for certainty, since so much seems to be
outside their sphere of control and changing, usually for
the worse. Their reaction to this change may be to
withdraw or to become cranky. Or, their reaction may
affect simple communication: a question asked to elderly people may go unanswered, not because of
deafness or being out of touch with reality, but because
they do not know the answer and decide not to respond
at all, thus avoiding yet another uncertainty.

Isolation. Being old and disabled brings on isolation, which can take a variety of forms. Quite often there is physical isolation; the elderly cannot get out and shop, visit, or go to a play. Isolation also results from sensory deprivation, from living in a radically changing world, from being treated as a biological instead of as a personal entity, and from being preoccupied with one's own body and feelings. Also, some of our older friends are simply ignored by their families, fellow church members, nurses, and acquaintances, who "just can't seem to get by." Being in the parlor of a retirement home, in the hall of a nursing home, or in the middle of a neighborhood is no guarantee against isolation.

Each of us has experienced some isolation and loneliness at some point in life. Magnify that experience and add to it the fact that the situation will never change for the better, and you'll begin to approach the experience of many invalid, elderly people.

Each of us is different. None of us will experience the same kind of loneliness and isolation or cope with it in the same way. However, some of us are more susceptible to loneliness than others. For example, elderly people who were forever surrounded by family and friends are more likely to suffer from loneliness than persons who lived their lives as singles.[11]

It is difficult to admit loneliness, even to ourselves. The elderly may never tell you or the other people around them that they are lonely. They may have tried to bury their loneliness so deeply that they are barely aware of its existence. Manifestations of it may come out in anger, complaints, bizarre behavior, clinging, physical illness, or depression.

Loneliness is a universal human experience. There is

always a gulf between us and other human beings. However, the added pressures and pains of being invalid and older make it even more difficult to fulfill the need for human community and intimacy.

Depersonalization. College students of the late 1960s screamed about being treated like numbers. Assembly-line workers suffer from boredom, frustration, and anger when they feel like nonessential cogs in a nonessential wheel. Likewise, the elderly also experience similar negative feelings.

A person who in younger years was able to make an active contribution of gifts and talents to the lives of other people may lose much self-worth when becoming an invalid. (Note that the word "invalid" literally means "not valid.") The retired Type-A personality businessman may find himself falling apart when he can no longer rush about "being productive." Our culture inculcates a need to achieve in order to justify existence. The worth of this attitude, however, is debatable.

Elderly people also lose self-respect when health-care workers treat them impersonally. Frequently needed medical procedures violate a person's airspace. For some, exposure of one's body to the opposite sex oversteps the bounds of propriety, yet hospitals, clinics, nursing homes, and doctors' offices demand such exposure as a matter of routine. It is easy for a person to become "a gall bladder," or "that total hip in Room 551."

Nursing homes can inflict an institutional neurosis on their residents. The residents can become regimented to a greater or lesser degree, giving up some freedom in return for a home, medical care, and three meals a day. Formerly self-sufficient people become dependent when living according to the schedules, procedures, and menu of a nursing home. One dear old friend described herself and her fellow nursing-home residents as "inmates."

Retirement homes can be much more subtle in their depersonalization. A clergy friend of mine once reflected on what it is like to serve a congregation in a resort/retirement area. "We have all these very able, very capable, formerly influential people here, but when they move here they disengage," he said. "They don't just move geographically; they move from a whole way of life." When people move to a retirement home, the same sort of disengagement occurs. Residents make themselves susceptible to having decisions made for them in return for security, meals, and the like.

Institutions vary in their ability and inclination to personalize their programs. Some are good at it, others are not. Some expend dollars, time, and energy to make a difference, others offer mere lip service. But even the best institutions present elderly people with change, regimentation, and, thus, some depersonalization.

However, being outside of an institution is no assurance of being free from depersonalization. An elderly person in a private home may have much freedom and integrity, or may be at the mercy of family, nurses, or housekeepers. Furthermore, during any kind of transition an elderly person's history and, therefore, identity, tend to be discarded. When Mrs. Smith moves to the nursing home, the fact that she once swam the English Channel is not of much concern to the staff; instead they are concerned with whether or not she will take her medication willingly. New neighbors do not remember the days when Mr. Johnson had the most beautiful yard in the city; as a result they do not understand his anger when their children walk through what is now a dandelion patch on his front lawn.

Depression. Depression, especially among the elderly, is a commonly misunderstood condition. While we use the word to describe the "low" feeling we experience from time to time, depression is actually a psychosomatic condition in that it manifests itself both psychologically and physically. Depression shows itself through feelings of powerlessness, loss of meaning, boredom, manipulative behavior, and the general "blahs," as well as through somatic symptoms, such as headaches, backaches, heart palpitations, ulcerative colitis, insomnia, constipation, diarrhea, and constant tiredness. Medical and psychiatric authorities tend to disagree as to the causes of depression, offering as possibilities emotional trauma, heredity, chemical imbalances, or a combination of many things. Treatments vary; physicians use psychotherapy, drugs, and electroconvulsive therapy. However, none of these treatments are necessarily used as a result of the physician's idea of what caused the disease.

Levels of depression vary in the elderly. If you encounter depression in your older friend, you will not be able to do anything directly about the physical aspects. However, your being open gives that person an important outlet for emotional expression.

SENILITY?

Certainly some disorientation in the elderly is due to physiological reasons. Sensory deprivation, Alzheimer's disease, and hardening of the arteries account for the incongruous statements and actions of many invalid and older people. Psychotropic drugs are bound to have some negative effects from time to time, as are medications that are aimed at other ailments, like high blood pressure. Strokes will also produce disorientation.

But there is, I believe, another reason an invalid and elderly person is often off in another world:

> I had not seen Mrs. S for a month. When I entered her room she immediately started telling me about a horrifying experience she had been through a few weeks before.
>
> I had a little stroke," she said. "I didn't know where I was. It lasted a few days, apparently, and the nurses and the repairman said that I was talking about all these things that I had been doing when I lived in Virginia. There was no way they could have known about all the things they told me I'd said unless I'd said them, so it must be true."
>
> We talked on for awhile about how frightening it is to lose some days. Then the conversation changed to some different subjects. All of a sudden Mrs. S looked up at me with a sort of "scared-child" look on her face and said, "I didn't have a stroke. I have been so lonely since I've been here. I've tried so hard to make this my home, to make it just like things were back in Virginia. It's been so hard on me. I've worked so hard, but it's been so sad. I didn't have a stroke. I just went a little crazy for a little while. It was a happier place, but now I'm back here again. I think it was because things had gotten so bad and it was God's way of giving me a little relief."

We may debate about whether Mrs. S's "little relief" was a gift from God. But it is clear that she believed her, pardon this clinical expression, "senile episode" to be the result of her pain, loneliness, isolation, depression, and inability to cope with change. The fact that she was rapidly losing her eyesight also may have contributed to her anxiety. Subsequent visits with Mrs. S and conversations with her physician made it clear to me that she had neither suffered a stroke nor was she experiencing hardening of the arteries.

A combination of any or all of the factors previously discussed in this chapter may force a person to opt for a reality more pleasant than the one most of us inhabit. At times all of us would like to be someplace else. Or, we may wish to live in another time and be surrounded by the people who are familiar to us even though they may have died decades ago. Some folks are given the gift of not having to cope with the present situation and all its details and minutiae. They, like Mrs. S, are given the gift of spending time in another reality.

Sadly, though, not all "other worlds" are happy ones. Even when disoriented your elderly friend may experience turmoil and agitation. Perhaps it is a rationalization to say that a person is more comfortable even in agitated disorientation. However, disorientation in the elderly is usually based on past events or situations which, if they have been successfully resolved, give a subconscious knowledge of survival. Furthermore, even if an elderly person's past is filled with loose ends, disorientation could provide a rare opportunity for some kind of resolution to occur. A rationalization? Perhaps. Perhaps not.

RELATIONSHIPS

The people with whom we spend the hours and minutes of our days can add to or detract from our growth as persons. Those people with whom the elderly have contact can provide them with enhancing experiences or they can very quietly and unintentionally sap them of emotional strength. Elderly people may have a large number of very frequent contacts, but that is no guarantee that their needs are being met. The quality of those contacts is what counts.

Different needs are met by different people. Even younger people in good health best find their needs met not by one but by several persons who comprise a system. You can better understand the elderly by spending time pondering the makeup of their system of relationships and by asking yourself which needs are met by which persons and which needs are going unmet. You will discover that family, contemporaries, younger friends, medical personnel, and other support-service persons are usually at the center of the elderly's social system.

Family. No other single factor in our lives shapes who we are and who we become like our family does. Culture, education, vocation, friends, and pastimes are important, but through heredity and conditioning, families affect our every aspect. In the family relationship we gain our outlook on life and its meaning. In families we develop patterns of relating to other people and to the world. These outlooks and patterns are established through years of experiences with parents, siblings, spouses, and children.

In the family lines of authority, whether spoken or unspoken, are drawn and lived with. Responsibility is sensed and lived out. Ways of expressing love and affection are learned, modified to suit the particular personalities involved, and then passed on to subsequent generations. Even the manner in which conflict is handled is "inherited" by children.

As a person becomes older and more dependent, as health loses its vibrancy, the relationship between parents and children undergoes changes. Over a span of a few years, or even weeks, forty to fifty years of firmly established ways of relating undergo radical transformation. Father, who has been "the law" and the bastion of strength for the family, becomes an invalid, unable to care for himself. His daughter, who has always treated him in the way that daughters treat fathers, out of necessity takes over the parenting role. Changes like these take their toll on all family members.

Parents spend years as the authorities, the responsible parties, the judges, the comforters. Then the situation and the roles all change. At times it is a gradual process, which allows adjustment to take place without too much shock to the parent or to the child. But gradual change can contribute to real issues being hidden and to a lack of awareness to what is occurring.

On the other hand, acute change often surfaces the sources of problems, but it can also be overwhelming. Immediate concern for safety or for medical care holds sway over seemingly less immediate issues of happiness or emotional hurt. Correct medical care is something we can see; happiness and emotional growth are intangibles. When those intangible issues are finally addressed, we chance hearing answers we don't particularly want to hear.

Parents and children experience a wide range of feelings when roles reverse and the children become care givers instead of care receivers. When mother moves to a nursing home, her children go through a great deal of turmoil. Even though all the facts dictate a nursing home, the children may still feel guilt about "putting mother away" and anger over their own helplessness to resolve the situation in any other way. Also, children often bear the brunt of a parent's anger because of an attitude of "they put me here and wouldn't take me into their home" on the part of an institutionalized parent.

Despite the care that a parent would receive in an institution, "the nursing home represents the ultimate personal failure for the elderly and their family."[12] Families add to the problem when they deny the reality of this difficult situation with statements like "This is a lovely home here. See the pretty flowers."

The entry of a parent into a retirement complex has fewer problems. Usually such a person is still mobile, in relatively good health, and has chosen, for a variety of reasons, to live in the complex. Perhaps friends live there. Or, perhaps it seems life will be more carefree without having a yard to keep up. Also, a retirement complex presents a modicum of independence from children. Finally, if the residence offers nursing care it eliminates an elderly person's fear of having to move later to some unknown, unfamiliar world.

Elderly people who live in their own homes can also be a cause of concern to their children. Their safety and security must be taken care of as well as their needs for shopping and transportation. Fulfilling these needs falls upon the children, often invading their lives.

Sometimes the elderly and their children will share a house. This situation presents its own unique joys and problems for all parties involved. Ideally, problem issues should be faced well before any real need for such a living arrangement exists. Practically, however, this is not always possible. And, even after surfacing the "hottest" issues, more will arise. The abilities to raise issues as they surface, to allow for adequate airing of feelings and opinions, and to negotiate amicable solutions are necessary for a happy situation. Scheduling quarterly evaluation sessions might help to enhance the process.

Parents, children, and grandchildren all need privacy. If a parent has to share a bedroom with a grandchild, special allowances for privacy need to be made in order to compensate. For example, grandma might be allowed to dress in private or to have her morning coffee alone in the room, while granddaughter has sole rights to the room in the late afternoon, before supper. The bathroom traffic jam each morning might need some monitoring in order to allow all members of the family adequate access. Some arrangements might be made about the family's eating format. Perhaps once or twice a week granddad could dine alone to give him and his progeny a little distance.

Some freedom of choice in life style and schedule needs to exist. The parent might be given the right to entertain friends for cards or dinner. The issue of whether or not the elderly parent has responsibility for baby-sitting the grandchildren, or vice versa, needs to be clearly spelled out.

Precisely negotiated financial arrangements are necessary to prevent feelings of being burdened or causing burden. When reviewed periodically, they can lead to discussions of other areas of the live-in relationship.

Though it sounds very legal and cold, working out an informal contract on all aspects of home sharing can avoid much hurt and misunderstanding down the road. Honesty in expressing wishes and a commitment to working out solutions are worth the difficulty they are to attain.

People with an increasingly dependent elderly parent experience intense, mixed feelings. Seeking help from an objective third party or talking with another person who has had a similar experience can provide relief from

the sense of guilt that children usually experience. The
fear is that we are hurting our parent in some way, yet
the truth usually is that we do not take care of ourselves
enough. Somehow we expect to be superhuman and
able to handle all things well, possessing some kind of
magic wand that can erase all pain and difficulty. Standing back from the situation from time to time can mean
a clearer vision of both our parent's needs and our own
needs. From that vision we can plan strategy and tactics
in caring for our father or mother. We can see some of
the dynamics of the reversal from being the care receiver
to being the care giver. What can at first seem cold and
calculating in our managing of a parent's life can then be
seen as the act of love it truly is. It is, perhaps, unfair to
think of your life as not *including* your invalid parent; it
is not unfair to think of it as not being totally *controlled*
and *determined* by that parent.

All families are different, just as all individuals within
families are different. Working out the details of how
those differences affect our own situations is a task
before us all.

Contemporaries. Having old friends nearby may be a
source of comfort and strength to your elderly friend.
Shared history — having suffered through crises
together, having mutually important joyous times —
provides a strong bond between two people. However,
increasing frailty, decreasing mobility, and, ultimately,
death stand in the way of contemporaries being assured
of that bond being a continued source of strength.
Friends experience grief when they see each other
weaken in body or in mind. In addition, the fact that
two persons have been friends for a long time is no
guarantee that the relationship will continue. As per-

sons change, needs and interests change. We cannot assume that when elderly people are surrounded by others with whom they share a long history that they are going to be in a more settled and stable situation.

Between Generations. Some of our older friends will have frequent contact with persons of all ages while others will be limited to one or two age groups. Those with more limited exposure will live with a somewhat distorted view of the world and its people.

Change forces the elderly to make major adjustments. A retired nursery-school teacher deprived of sharing life with younger children will go through a difficult adjustment. Persons who have never had children but who end up in a setting where children are frequently present find they either have to retreat or change.

Young folks caroling in institutions during the holiday season present a unique situation for interaction between visitors and residents. A viewer observing the dynamics can find it to be a greatly magnified study of the whole range of human relationships.

Medical Personnel. Because of the physiological aspects of aging, your older friend will have many contacts with the medical community, either through private doctors' offices, hospitals, or nursing homes.

Physicians who care for invalid and elderly patients have a difficult job. Doctors are trained to cure and heal, and not much curing and healing can be done with the aging process. Also, it is easy for medical personnel to stereotype. For the physician time can seem more valuably spent on the young and vibrant. When taking a medical history, the doctor can find the elderly patient vague and drifting; the process is often lengthier simply because older persons have longer histories![13] One physician friend said, "It's one thing to hear, 'When I was five years old,' from a twenty-five-year-old. It's quite another thing to ponder the length of the history taking when the patient who is seventy begins with her health at age five."

Since older people's bodies are changing so rapidly, diagnosis can be difficult. Frequently the patient suffers from multiple diseases and conditions. Home remedies may cloak symptoms. Sometimes the patient's fear of diagnosis may result in only partial revelation of symptoms. It is natural, then, that many physicians have a difficult time with older patients.

Relationships with medical personnel can cause different sorts of reactions in the elderly. One person may fear them, another may become emotionally overdependent on them, calling too frequently and in unnecessary situations. The hospital may become symbolic of decline, or it may be seen as a place of relief from both physical pain and the pain of loneliness.

Other Support Persons. Other people important in the care of your older friend may include housekeepers, trust officers, or kindly neighbors. These persons may bear the brunt of your friend's anger or depression, or they may be the recipients of much love and kindness. It is important to remember that each support person, though providing important care and attention, may be a symbol of your friend's growing dependence. Thus, learning who these helpers are will help you understand more and more about your friend's total well-being.

Your older friend lives life in a network of relationships. They may be healthy and happy relationships which add to your friend's wholeness and sense of well-being, or they may be rocky and marked by unsatisfying times. Discussions with your friend can yield much knowledge about this area.

SPIRITUALITY

Listening to your older friend for expressions of belief and values may allow you to enter into some important discussions about life's meaning. Naturally, people have very different heritages and outlooks. One person will offer no religious data, another some beliefs that are a help in a crisis, a third understandings of God that cause difficulties in putting together the meaning of what is presently being experienced.

Our basic tendency to provide answers means that we must instead provide space for that other person, allowing for full expression and "owning" of beliefs. We must resist the urge to correct and modify according to what seems to make sense to us. After all, what makes sense to us may not make any sense to another person.

It is often incorrectly assumed that the invalid and elderly person is more religious than the general populace.[14] Conversation with the elderly may include talk of church groups that come for visits, but the reason for such a religious topic is clear: the visit was an event that helped pass the time or made the person feel special. An elderly person may avidly discuss reading the Bible or watching religious television shows because these are outlets which may have become important because of decreased mobility.[15] No longer can an older person get in the car and run down to the church to study or worship or volunteer.

The fact that the elderly may be very immobile means that they are all the more susceptible to invasions of religious privacy by individuals and groups. The following conversation is a good example of this.

> "They came in here and said that if I *really* believed, then I'd get better and could walk out of here. What do you think?" She looked both angry and puzzled.
>
> "It sounds as though they were saying that your illness is your fault, that somehow you caused it." I awaited her response, a little nervous.
>
> "Yeah, it does. They're wrong. Dead wrong." (I relaxed a little.) "But when you're lying here, anybody in the world can walk in here and impose their views on you, and sometimes you get so you almost believe them."

Thus, you can see from this example that the space you offer a person for spirituality is vitally important.

The person you visit is made up of a unique, miraculous combination of aspects. Injury or problems with any one of those aspects affects the others, either positively or negatively. You are caring for a total person. Whatever that person says or communicates to you is set before you for your understanding and, hopefully, for your responses of love. Though what you have just read may seem technical or complicated, use it to realize the complexity of the unique person for whom you care. Use it to help you get through the barriers that stand in the way of generating communication that can result in the meeting of souls.

Your Time Together

TIME WITH your older friend can be a shallow, hurried, fleeting experience, or it can be a deep experience, filled with love. You might feel a little nobler after visiting your friend, or you might leave feeling frustrated. Similarly, your elderly friend might be no better from your visit, or your visit might have been the most extraordinary forty minutes of your friend's week. The difference lies in how you use that time and how you allow that time to flow. It lies in whether you allow your friend to act naturally and to speak from the heart and mind. Ultimately, your time together will be determined by whether or not your elderly friend perceives you as an accepting human being, a person who can respond with love and care.

LOGISTICS

It is a good idea to make an appointment for your time together. This is both courteous and therapeutic for older people. Half the fun of a vacation or of a holiday is the anticipation and preparation beforehand. Give the elderly, who most likely get no vacation or holiday, the pleasure of anticipating your presence. They may enjoy gathering their thoughts ahead of time, and when you arrive you may find some goodies or some interesting photographs or cards set out for you.

Spontaneously dropping by is fine at times, though

you may run into activities, beauty-shop appointments, or treatments. But an unplanned visit deprives your friend of being able to anticipate having a guest. Also, different people have different biological clocks. Popping by in the morning may yield a very different experience from your regular afternoon visit to an afternoon person. Unscheduled visits do not have the same sort of feel to them as do visits in which you have intentionally carved out and planned a time together.

The Christmas season floods nursing and retirement homes with well-wishers. For many residents the carolers are a welcome change from routine and a happy reminder of the holiday season. For other residents these people are an intrusion. "Where are they the other fifty weeks of the year? Why don't they feel guilty enough to come then?" a friend once asked me. Knowing how the deluge of people affects your older friend will help you in scheduling your own time together. If your friend loves all the mayhem, then you might want to slack off a little. If it is bothersome, you may wish to spend some very quiet and personal time together.

You must decide how often and how long you can visit with your older friend. If you follow a schedule, you will not have to worry about conflicts. If you know when you will be finished with your visit, the question as to whether or not you will get to school to pick up that car pool has been answered. You should realize that no one ever keeps you longer than you can stay, and that, if you stay past your schedule, you are keeping yourself. If visits become unpleasant because they turn into marathons, you can change that. Stick to your schedule! It will make you a better friend and listener because you won't be worried about being detained.

When you are away make the mails your visiting

tool. Even friends with poor eyesight will find someone to read your note out loud — maybe even three or four times! Also, notes confirming your next meeting will provide a reference point for people who are forgetful about information shared over the phone.

Gifts are wonderful things because they are tangible expressions of our care and concern. We may feel more at ease when we arrive with something in our hands. But gifts should be tools of the relationship and not its essence. Anyone can bring a gift; only you can bring you.

The nature of gifts should be carefully considered. Gifts with sharp points or edges may not be safe. Flowers that smell lovely to you may not be welcome to your friend, since they are only a reminder of not being able to smell at all. Gifts of food can present a problem if there are diet restrictions. One nursing home resident was given a beautiful basket of apples, but he had no teeth. The staff ended up eating the apples. Some people would have enjoyed giving those apples away. This elderly man didn't.

If your older friend is not someone with whom you have had a close relationship, you are faced with the dilemma of how to address that person. Should you use first name or last name? For a woman should you say Mrs., Miss, or Ms.? Whatever comes naturally is best, though you may want to ask directly just to be sure.

SHARING YOURSELF

Your visits are times to allow your older friend to be him- or herself. The way you present yourself may determine whether or not your friend feels able to respond. We make ourselves unavailable, even when standing next to a person, in a variety of subtle ways. Our posture, the way we listen or fail to listen, the direction in which we face, all of these factors either add to or detract from the image of availability we project.

Be aware of how you enter the physical surroundings in which you find your older friend, for your entry could set the tone for the entire visit. Rushing into the room may show your excitement in being there or it may startle your friend. Furthermore, keep in mind the fact that you are in that person's home. Rearranging the flowers may be a violation of that person's territory.

Where and how you station yourself in the room may also affect your ability to communicate. If you stand you may project an image of being in a hurry. Towering over your friend can also connote an unequal relationship. When you sit be aware of your posture, taking into account the physical infirmities of the person you are visiting. Ask yourself questions like these: Am I too far away for him to see me through those cataracts? Is there a bright light that may interfere with her vision? Is he able to turn his head and body to see me? Do I look tired or bored sitting in this position? Finally, facing someone as we speak is a common courtesy which is especially important when dealing with persons whose hearing may be impaired.

Your relationship will grow if you give your friend the opportunity to speak clearly and fully. This means listening to what the older person is saying, thinking, and feeling. It does not mean thinking of what you are going to say next, nor does it have anything to do with that dinner party you are planning for next week or the soap opera playing on the television across from you.

Listening must be practiced! Good listening consists of several levels: (1) noting what information or data is being shared; (2) noting what that information or data means to the sharer; and (3) noting the feeling level of the sharer. The best kind of listening has you getting inside the skin of other people, making the issues they face your issues, making the pain they feel your pain, making the joy or resolve they experience your joy and resolve as well. This very involved kind of listening will help you understand your elderly friend's confusion, doubt, despair, or satisfaction with life.

Our eyes must be at work in the listening process. Facial expressions, body posture, and other actions give clues as to how the other person is thinking and feeling and living. Noting changes between visits can provide information concerning the elderly person's present state. Ask yourself questions like these: When he feels good is he in a wheelchair and when he feels bad in a bed? Has the neatness of her clothing changed since last time? Are there pictures or mementos that have appeared since I last visited?

You need to let the other person determine how your time together will be spent. It may be your friend's only chance to determine the drift of things; everything else may be determined by others. Your friend may want the time together to involve chitchat, handholding, playing twenty questions, reading, or silence. Whatever the case, don't make the decision on your own accord. It is not asking too much to let your friend determine the direction of your visit. There may be no other person who gives that opportunity.

SPENDING QUALITY TIME TOGETHER

Spending time with an older person does not mean that you become a nonentity. You have opportunities in a

visit to respond, but you must be careful with those opportunities. We most often violate territory by feeling
we have to respond prematurely or in a certain way. For
example, we often feel compelled to respond with words
when words might not be necessary.

First and foremost, our responses should be means by
which we maintain the other person's integrity. Reflective counseling techniques, in which what the person
has just said is restated in question form, are frequently
helpful. Use of these techniques helps make certain that
we have understood very clearly what our friend has
said. The questions we ask can be rephrased somewhat,
or they can jump one step further in order to try and
establish a deeper significance to what the person has
said. For example, the comment "This room is always
too hot" can be questioned in many ways: It's always
too hot in this room? Too hot in here all the time? Are
you tired of the way they run this place? Mad at the
manager again? You have no control over the heat or
anything else in here?

This way of responding has several desirable ends.
First, you are given a means by which to ascertain that
what the person said is what you heard. It is difficult to
understand the speech of certain invalid and elderly
people, especially those who have suffered strokes. The
questioning method keeps you on the same wavelength.
Second, the person with whom you are speaking is
assured of having communicated correctly and of having someone hear that communication. One person in
the whole wide world knows! For a person who is feeling lonely and alienated this experience can be so special
and important that it can help build the closest trust.
Not only do you know what your friend is thinking and

feeling, your friend knows you know! Third, you remain nonjudgmental. The person's integrity, beliefs, and feelings are given a valid hearing. This is meat to people who have become dependent upon others who either ignore, deny, or try to change the last enclaves of a person's identity, one's thoughts and feelings. Fourth, the person you are spending your time with gets to determine the agenda, how the time is spent. Finally, your friend may hear things in new ways, bringing an awareness of thoughts and feelings previously unknown.

I had several counseling sessions with one hospital patient who was particularly ripe for reflective techniques. During the sessions I offered no words of wisdom or judgmental or evaluative input. Everything that was expressed came originally from him. A week later I received a lovely note thanking me for "all you have done for me in helping me come to grips with my illness" when, in fact, he had had the resources within himself to cope with his crisis. I was merely an agent for him to hear himself in a new way.

However, these techniques do have a danger to them. It is too easy to think of oneself as a parrot or an echo. The task is to focus on understanding or discovering that other person while at the same time letting that person voluntarily open up for your discovery. Naturally, there are times to use reflective techniques and times to discard them. Sometimes plain old small talk or a discussion on an important issue of the day is more in order. But too often small talk and conversations centered on outside issues can become escapes or ways to avoid the important issue of being together.

Of course the spoken word is not the only response

that you can make. Touching may also be a way to respond. From birth we are cuddled and loved in a series
of important touches. In illness or infirmity, especially
in an institution, those touches are replaced by treatment. Touching is done to manage a patient instead of
to communicate affection or concern. Invalids, who are
affectionate, sexual human beings, are deprived of that
which for them was normative.

Other nonverbals may also be appropriate responses.
Facial expressions can arise from our hearts. Tears are
even appropriate at times. They can be instruments in
sharing love and care for another person in a crisis.

Responses may involve sharing an opinion or two.
Caution is prescribed here; make certain that you have
understood what the person has said — and be sure you
were asked for an opinion! Opinions set before us the
trap of moving the agenda for our time together out of
the realm of the immediate and into the realm of the im-
personal. There is a difference between sharing an opinion and sharing a feeling.

Your response to your older friend may involve an
aspect of rehabilitation for that person. An invalid cut
off from the outside world suffers from sensory deprivation and from a variety of other conditions which can
result in disorientation. It is debatable whether or not a
person who is severely disoriented ought to be faced
with trying to readjust to the normal world, but there
are situations that may call for some rehabilitative
work on your part. This work should begin only after
you have spent much time with the person, building
trust, and have gotten to know the situation well.

Casual reorientation techniques might include stating
your name, the day, date, and time as you enter: "Hello,

Edna. It's Mary Smith again. I'm here on Thursday, June 27, at 1:30, just like I said." Noting Edna's reaction to this kind of stimulus will give you an indication whether she is agitated or put at ease by the information.

In more structured orientation work, creativity and sensitivity are demanded. I remember one visitor who worked with her older friend using photographs of his family. The confused gentleman eventually recalled all their names. When his family drove eighty miles to visit him in the nursing home one day, he surprised them by greeting them by name. Soon thereafter his family found a space for him in a nursing home nearer to where they lived. There had to be a connection between the gentleman's restored recognition and his family's desire to have him nearby. (Incidentally, the visitor was shocked one day to find that the gentleman remembered her name as well!) We can only guess as to the importance of that visitor's work when viewed through the eyes of the gentleman and his family.

Your visit can be a very important time in the life of your older friend. Not much happens to the elderly person that you and I would call special. But your visit can provide opportunity for something special to happen.

Plan for that visit. Work out the details of time, parameters, and frequency. Open yourself during the visit. Create a space for your friend, a territory in which, by shaping the time you offer, your friend can act naturally. Then respond in ways that are both honest and life-enhancing.

As the special nature of your time together grows for your older friend, it will grow in beauty for you too.

Filling Your Cup

You would not want to go to a doctor who did not use every resource possible to take the best care of you. Nor would you like to be educated by a teacher whose education and training were miserably out of date. Likewise, you can help your older friend — and yourself — by continuing to increase your knowledge about the elderly.

Previously I mentioned that you can continue to learn through reading and through reflection. I recommend that you use people resources as well. There may be a member of the clergy or a social worker who has a special interest in aging. Some physicians or nurses can be good information sources as well as good listeners for those times when you need to talk. Spending time with others who share the same kinds of experiences may also be helpful, either as part of a formal support program or as an informal "let's have lunch together" sort of sharing.

The point is clear: you do not have to go it alone.

Notes

THE ELDERLY'S ENVIRONMENT

1. C. Davis Hendricks and Jon Hendricks, *Aging in Mass Society: Myths and Realities* (Cambridge, Mass.: Winthrop Publishers, 1977), 281.

2. Eva Boaz Kahana, "Health Care Facilities," in *The Care of the Geriatric Patient*, ed. E. V. Cowdry and Franz U. Steinberg (St. Louis, Mo.: C. V. Mosby Co., 1971), 465.

3. Ibid., 457.

4. Ibid.

5. Hendricks and Hendricks, *Aging in Mass Society*, 281.

6. Ibid.

7. Ibid.

8. D. Wedderburn, "The Aged and Society," in *Textbook of Geriatric Medicine and Gerontology*, ed. J. C. Brocklehurst (London: Churchill Livingstone, 1973), 708.

OUR OLDER FRIENDS

1. W. F. Anderson, "Preventive Medicine in Old Age," in *Textbook of Geriatric Medicine and Gerontology*, ed. J. C. Brocklehurst (London: Churchill Livingstone, 1973), 721.

2. Antoinette Bosco, *What Do We Really Know About Aging?* (Albany: State University of New York Press, 1977), 25.

3. Ibid., 27.

4. Hendricks and Hendricks, *Aging in Mass Society*, 135.

5. Martha Storandt, "Psychologic Aspects," in *The Care of the Geriatric Patient*, ed. E. V. Cowdry and Franz U. Steinberg (St. Louis, Mo.: C. V. Mosby Co., 1976), 322.

6. Ibid.

7. Hendricks, *Aging in Mass Society*, 155.

8. Kahana, "Health Care Facilities," 464.

9. Ibid., 465.

10. Hendricks and Hendricks, *Aging in Mass Society*, 275.

11. Ibid., 298.

12. Ibid., 282.

13. Franz V. Steinberg, "The Evaluation and Treatment of the Geriatric Patient: General Considerations," in *The Care of the Geriatric Patient*, ed. E. V. Cowdry and Franz U. Steinberg (St. Louis, Mo.: C. V. Mosby Co., 1976), 4.

14. Hendricks and Hendricks, *Aging in Mass Society*, 314.

15. Ibid., 315.

Bibliography

Anderson, W. F. "Preventive Medicine in Old Age." In *Textbook of Geriatric Medicine and Gerontology*, edited by J. C. Brocklehurst. London: Churchill Livingstone, 1973.

Birren, James E., et al. "Introduction to the Study of Human Aging." In *Human Aging*. Washington, D.C.: U.S. Government Printing Office.

Blank, Paul, et al. "Social Psychological Characteristics of Old Age." In *Human Aging*. Washington, D.C.: U. S. Government Printing Office.

Bosco, Antoinette. *What Do We Really Know About Aging?* Albany: State University of New York Press, 1977.

Burger, Sarah Greene, and Martha D'Erasmo. *Living in a Nursing Home: A Complete Guide for Residents, Their Families and Friends.* New York: Seabury Press, 1976.

Caird, F. I., and T. G. Judge. *Assessment of the Elderly Patient.* Tunbridge Wells, U. K.: Pitman Medical Publishing Co., 1977.

Clinebell, Howard. *Basic Types of Pastoral Counseling.* Nashville: Abingdon Press, 1966.

Ernst, Marvin, and Herbert Shore. *Sensitizing People to the Processes of Aging: The In-Service Educator's Guide.* Denton: North Texas State University, 1977.

Hendricks, C. Davis, and Jon Hendricks. *Aging in Mass Society: Myths and Realities.* Cambridge, Mass.: Winthrop Publishers, 1977.

Kahana, Eva Boaz. "Health Care Facilities." In *The Care of the Geriatric Patient*, edited by E. V. Cowdry and Franz U. Steinberg. St. Louis, Mo.: C. V. Mosby Co., 1976.

Kübler-Ross, Elisabeth. *On Death and Dying.* New York: Macmillan Co., 1969.

Munnicks, Joep, and Arthur Bogot. "Psychology of Aging." In *Textbook of Geriatric Medicine and Gerontology*, edited by J. C. Brocklehurst. London: Churchill Livingstone, 1973.

Nouwen, Henri J. *Reaching Out: The Three Movements of Spiritual Life.* New York: Doubleday & Co., 1975.

_____. *The Wounded Healer: Ministry in Contemporary Society.* Garden City, N.Y.: Doubleday & Co., 1972.

Nouwen, Henri J., et al. *Aging: The Fulfillment of Life.* New York: Doubleday & Co., 1976.

Steinberg, Franz U. "The Evaluation and Treatment of the Geriatric Patient." In *The Care of the Geriatric Patient*, edited by E. V. Cowdry and Franz U. Steinberg. St. Louis, Mo.: C. V. Mosby Co., 1976.

Storandt, Martha. "Psychologic Aspects." In *The Care of the Geriatric Patient*, edited by E. V. Cowdry and Franz U. Steinberg. St. Louis, Mo.: C. V. Mosby Co., 1976.

Tulloch, Janet. *A Home Is Not a Home: Life Within a Nursing Home.* New York: Seabury Press, 1976.

Wedderburn, D. "The Aged and Society." In *Textbook of Geriatric Medicine and Gerontology*, edited by J. C. Brocklehurst. London: Churchill Livingstone, 1973.

Westberg, Granger. *Good Grief.* Philadelphia: Fortress Press, 1962.